ISBN 0-7935-3965-X

7777 W. BLUEMOUND RD. P.O. BOX 13819 MILWAUKEE, WI 53213

—

SILENT NIGHT

Arrangement by
MARIAH CAREY

ALL I WANT FOR CHRISTMAS IS YOU

Words and Music by MARIAH CAREY
and WALTER AFANASIEFF

O HOLY NIGHT

Arrangement by MARIAH CAREY
and WALTER AFANASIEFF

*2nd time, sung 8va to 2nd ending.

CHRISTMAS
(BABY PLEASE COME HOME)

Words and Music by PHIL SPECTOR,
ELLIE GREENWICH and JEFF BARRY

but it's not like Christ - mas at all. _____

'Cause I re - mem - ber when ___ you were here _____

and all the fun we had _____ last year. _____

(Christ - mas) Pret - ty lights ___ on the tree, _____
Instrumental solo
(Christ - mas) If there ___ was a way _____

MISS YOU MOST
AT CHRISTMAS TIME

Words and Music by MARIAH CAREY
and WALTER AFANASIEFF

Woo;

The fire is burn - ing, the
gaze out the win - dow this

room's all a - glow, _____ out - side the De - cem - ber wind
cold win - ter's night _____ at all of the twin - kle - ing

28

JOY TO THE WORLD

Words and Music by HOYT AXTON
Arrangement by MARIAH CAREY
and WALTER AFANASIEFF

34

BORN ON THIS DAY

Words and Music by MARIAH CAREY
and WALTER AFANASIEFF

SANTA CLAUS IS COMIN' TO TOWN

Words and Music by HAVEN GILLESPIE
and J. FRED COOTS

44

HARK THE HERALD ANGELS SING/
GLORIA (IN EXCELSIS DEO)

Arrangement by MARIAH CAREY,
WALTER AFANASIEFF and LORIS HOLLAND

JESUS WHAT A WONDERFUL CHILD

Arrangement by MARIAH CAREY,
WALTER AFANASIEFF and LORIS HOLLAND